Welcon
Your Daily, Weekl
Cleaning F

GW01451289

Being Organized will help to make Cleaning your House as Stress Free and Efficient as possible.

With Daily, Weekly and Monthly Check Lists, you will soon have your housework and cleaning schedule running smoothly and effectively.

In Case of Loss, Please Contact:

Name:

Contact Number:

Email:

My Daily Cleaning Check List

WEEK BEGINNING:

DAILY TASK:	MON	TUES	WED	THURS	FRI	SAT	SUN

DATES TO REMEMBER THIS WEEK:

CLEANING SUPPLIES NEEDED:

My Weekly Cleaning Check List

Monday – Cleaning Tasks	✔

Tuesday – Cleaning Tasks	✔

Wednesday – Cleaning Tasks	✔

Thursday – Cleaning Tasks	✔

NOTES:

_____

_____

_____

_____

My Weekly Cleaning Check List

Friday – Cleaning Tasks	✓

Saturday – Cleaning Tasks	✓

Sunday – Cleaning Tasks	✓

Plans for Next Week:

NOTES:

_____

_____

_____

_____

My Weekly Cleaning Check List

This Weeks' To Do List:

1)
2)
3)
4)
5)

My Personal Goals This Week:

My Daily Cleaning Check List

WEEK BEGINNING:

DAILY TASK:	MON	TUES	WED	THURS	FRI	SAT	SUN

DATES TO REMEMBER THIS WEEK:

CLEANING SUPPLIES NEEDED:

My Weekly Cleaning Check List

Monday – Cleaning Tasks	✔

Tuesday – Cleaning Tasks	✔

Wednesday – Cleaning Tasks	✔

Thursday – Cleaning Tasks	✔

NOTES:

_____

_____

_____

_____

My Weekly Cleaning Check List

Friday – Cleaning Tasks	✓

Saturday – Cleaning Tasks	✓

Sunday – Cleaning Tasks	✓

Plans for Next Week:

NOTES:

My Weekly Cleaning Check List

This Weeks' To Do List:

1)	
2)	
3)	
4)	
5)	

My Personal Goals This Week:

My Daily Cleaning Check List

WEEK BEGINNING:

DAILY TASK:	MON	TUES	WED	THURS	FRI	SAT	SUN

DATES TO REMEMBER THIS WEEK:

CLEANING SUPPLIES NEEDED:

My Weekly Cleaning Check List

Monday – Cleaning Tasks	✔

Tuesday – Cleaning Tasks	✔

Wednesday – Cleaning Tasks	✔

Thursday – Cleaning Tasks	✔

NOTES:

_____

_____

_____

_____

My Weekly Cleaning Check List

Friday – Cleaning Tasks	✔

Saturday – Cleaning Tasks	✔

Sunday – Cleaning Tasks	✔

Plans for Next Week:

NOTES:

My Weekly Cleaning Check List

This Weeks' To Do List:

1)
2)
3)
4)
5)

My Personal Goals This Week:

My Daily Cleaning Check List

WEEK BEGINNING:

DAILY TASK:	MON	TUES	WED	THURS	FRI	SAT	SUN

DATES TO REMEMBER THIS WEEK:

CLEANING SUPPLIES NEEDED:

My Weekly Cleaning Check List

Monday – Cleaning Tasks	✓

Tuesday – Cleaning Tasks	✓

Wednesday – Cleaning Tasks	✓

Thursday – Cleaning Tasks	✓

NOTES:

_____

_____

_____

_____

My Weekly Cleaning Check List

Friday – Cleaning Tasks	✔

Saturday – Cleaning Tasks	✔

Sunday – Cleaning Tasks	✔

Plans for Next Week:

NOTES:

My Weekly Cleaning Check List

This Weeks' To Do List:

1)
2)
3)
4)
5)

My Personal Goals This Week:

My Daily Cleaning Check List

WEEK BEGINNING:

DAILY TASK:	MON	TUES	WED	THURS	FRI	SAT	SUN

DATES TO REMEMBER THIS WEEK:

CLEANING SUPPLIES NEEDED:

My Weekly Cleaning Check List

Monday – Cleaning Tasks	✓

Tuesday – Cleaning Tasks	✓

Wednesday – Cleaning Tasks	✓

Thursday – Cleaning Tasks	✓

NOTES:

_____

_____

_____

_____

My Weekly Cleaning Check List

Friday – Cleaning Tasks	✓

Saturday – Cleaning Tasks	✓

Sunday – Cleaning Tasks	✓

Plans for Next Week:

NOTES:

_____

_____

_____

_____

My Weekly Cleaning Check List

This Weeks' To Do List:

1)
2)
3)
4)
5)

My Personal Goals This Week:

My Daily Cleaning Check List

WEEK BEGINNING:

DAILY TASK:	MON	TUES	WED	THURS	FRI	SAT	SUN

DATES TO REMEMBER THIS WEEK:

CLEANING SUPPLIES NEEDED:

My Weekly Cleaning Check List

Monday – Cleaning Tasks	✔

Tuesday – Cleaning Tasks	✔

Wednesday – Cleaning Tasks	✔

Thursday – Cleaning Tasks	✔

NOTES:

_____

_____

_____

_____

My Weekly Cleaning Check List

Friday – Cleaning Tasks	✔

Saturday – Cleaning Tasks	✔

Sunday – Cleaning Tasks	✔

Plans for Next Week:

NOTES:

My Weekly Cleaning Check List

This Weeks' To Do List:

1)
2)
3)
4)
5)

My Personal Goals This Week:

My Daily Cleaning Check List

WEEK BEGINNING:

DAILY TASK:	MON	TUES	WED	THURS	FRI	SAT	SUN

DATES TO REMEMBER THIS WEEK:

CLEANING SUPPLIES NEEDED:

My Weekly Cleaning Check List

Monday – Cleaning Tasks	✔

Tuesday – Cleaning Tasks	✔

Wednesday – Cleaning Tasks	✔

Thursday – Cleaning Tasks	✔

NOTES:

_____

_____

_____

_____

My Weekly Cleaning Check List

Friday – Cleaning Tasks	✓

Saturday – Cleaning Tasks	✓

Sunday – Cleaning Tasks	✓

Plans for Next Week:

NOTES:

My Weekly Cleaning Check List

This Weeks' To Do List:

1)
2)
3)
4)
5)

My Personal Goals This Week:

My Daily Cleaning Check List

WEEK BEGINNING:

DAILY TASK:	MON	TUES	WED	THURS	FRI	SAT	SUN

DATES TO REMEMBER THIS WEEK:

CLEANING SUPPLIES NEEDED:

My Weekly Cleaning Check List

Monday – Cleaning Tasks	✓

Tuesday – Cleaning Tasks	✓

Wednesday – Cleaning Tasks	✓

Thursday – Cleaning Tasks	✓

NOTES:

_____

_____

_____

_____

My Weekly Cleaning Check List

Friday – Cleaning Tasks	✓

Saturday – Cleaning Tasks	✓

Sunday – Cleaning Tasks	✓

Plans for Next Week:

NOTES:
_____

_____

_____

_____

My Weekly Cleaning Check List

This Weeks' To Do List:

1)
2)
3)
4)
5)

My Personal Goals This Week:

My Daily Cleaning Check List

WEEK BEGINNING:

DAILY TASK:	MON	TUES	WED	THURS	FRI	SAT	SUN

DATES TO REMEMBER THIS WEEK:

CLEANING SUPPLIES NEEDED:

My Weekly Cleaning Check List

Monday – Cleaning Tasks	✓

Tuesday – Cleaning Tasks	✓

Wednesday – Cleaning Tasks	✓

Thursday – Cleaning Tasks	✓

NOTES:

_____

_____

_____

_____

My Weekly Cleaning Check List

Friday – Cleaning Tasks	✓

Saturday – Cleaning Tasks	✓

Sunday – Cleaning Tasks	✓

Plans for Next Week:

NOTES:

My Weekly Cleaning Check List

This Weeks' To Do List:

1)
2)
3)
4)
5)

My Personal Goals This Week:

My Daily Cleaning Check List

WEEK BEGINNING:

DAILY TASK:	MON	TUES	WED	THURS	FRI	SAT	SUN

DATES TO REMEMBER THIS WEEK:

CLEANING SUPPLIES NEEDED:

My Weekly Cleaning Check List

Monday – Cleaning Tasks	✓

Tuesday – Cleaning Tasks	✓

Wednesday – Cleaning Tasks	✓

Thursday – Cleaning Tasks	✓

NOTES:

_____

_____

_____

_____

My Weekly Cleaning Check List

Friday – Cleaning Tasks	✔

Saturday – Cleaning Tasks	✔

Sunday – Cleaning Tasks	✔

Plans for Next Week:

NOTES:

My Weekly Cleaning Check List

This Weeks' To Do List:

1)	
2)	
3)	
4)	
5)	

My Personal Goals This Week:

My Daily Cleaning Check List

WEEK BEGINNING:

DAILY TASK:	MON	TUES	WED	THURS	FRI	SAT	SUN

DATES TO REMEMBER THIS WEEK:

CLEANING SUPPLIES NEEDED:

My Weekly Cleaning Check List

Monday – Cleaning Tasks	✓

Tuesday – Cleaning Tasks	✓

Wednesday – Cleaning Tasks	✓

Thursday – Cleaning Tasks	✓

NOTES:

_____

_____

_____

_____

My Weekly Cleaning Check List

Friday – Cleaning Tasks	✔

Saturday – Cleaning Tasks	✔

Sunday – Cleaning Tasks	✔

Plans for Next Week:

NOTES:

_____

_____

_____

_____

My Weekly Cleaning Check List

This Weeks' To Do List:

1)
2)
3)
4)
5)

My Personal Goals This Week:

My Daily Cleaning Check List

WEEK BEGINNING:

DAILY TASK:	MON	TUES	WED	THURS	FRI	SAT	SUN

DATES TO REMEMBER THIS WEEK:

CLEANING SUPPLIES NEEDED:

My Weekly Cleaning Check List

Monday – Cleaning Tasks	✓

Tuesday – Cleaning Tasks	✓

Wednesday – Cleaning Tasks	✓

Thursday – Cleaning Tasks	✓

NOTES:

_____

_____

_____

_____

My Weekly Cleaning Check List

Friday – Cleaning Tasks	✓

Saturday – Cleaning Tasks	✓

Sunday – Cleaning Tasks	✓

Plans for Next Week:

NOTES:

_____

_____

_____

_____

My Weekly Cleaning Check List

This Weeks' To Do List:

1)
2)
3)
4)
5)

My Personal Goals This Week:

My Daily Cleaning Check List

WEEK BEGINNING:

DAILY TASK:	MON	TUES	WED	THURS	FRI	SAT	SUN

DATES TO REMEMBER THIS WEEK:

CLEANING SUPPLIES NEEDED:

My Weekly Cleaning Check List

Monday – Cleaning Tasks	✓

Tuesday – Cleaning Tasks	✓

Wednesday – Cleaning Tasks	✓

Thursday – Cleaning Tasks	✓

NOTES:

_____

_____

_____

_____

My Weekly Cleaning Check List

Friday – Cleaning Tasks	✔

Saturday – Cleaning Tasks	✔

Sunday – Cleaning Tasks	✔

Plans for Next Week:

NOTES:

My Weekly Cleaning Check List

This Weeks' To Do List:

1)
2)
3)
4)
5)

My Personal Goals This Week:

My Daily Cleaning Check List

WEEK BEGINNING:

DAILY TASK:	MON	TUES	WED	THURS	FRI	SAT	SUN

DATES TO REMEMBER THIS WEEK:

CLEANING SUPPLIES NEEDED:

My Weekly Cleaning Check List

Monday – Cleaning Tasks	✓

Tuesday – Cleaning Tasks	✓

Wednesday – Cleaning Tasks	✓

Thursday – Cleaning Tasks	✓

NOTES:

_____

_____

_____

_____

My Weekly Cleaning Check List

Friday – Cleaning Tasks	✓

Saturday – Cleaning Tasks	✓

Sunday – Cleaning Tasks	✓

Plans for Next Week:

NOTES:

My Weekly Cleaning Check List

This Weeks' To Do List:

1)
2)
3)
4)
5)

My Personal Goals This Week:

My Daily Cleaning Check List

WEEK BEGINNING:

DAILY TASK:	MON	TUES	WED	THURS	FRI	SAT	SUN

DATES TO REMEMBER THIS WEEK:

CLEANING SUPPLIES NEEDED:

My Weekly Cleaning Check List

Monday – Cleaning Tasks	✓

Tuesday – Cleaning Tasks	✓

Wednesday – Cleaning Tasks	✓

Thursday – Cleaning Tasks	✓

NOTES:

_____

_____

_____

_____

My Weekly Cleaning Check List

Friday – Cleaning Tasks	✓

Saturday – Cleaning Tasks	✓

Sunday – Cleaning Tasks	✓

Plans for Next Week:

NOTES:

My Weekly Cleaning Check List

This Weeks' To Do List:

1)
2)
3)
4)
5)

My Personal Goals This Week:

My Daily Cleaning Check List

WEEK BEGINNING:

DAILY TASK:	MON	TUES	WED	THURS	FRI	SAT	SUN

DATES TO REMEMBER THIS WEEK:

CLEANING SUPPLIES NEEDED:

My Weekly Cleaning Check List

Monday – Cleaning Tasks	✓

Tuesday – Cleaning Tasks	✓

Wednesday – Cleaning Tasks	✓

Thursday – Cleaning Tasks	✓

NOTES:

_____

_____

_____

_____

My Weekly Cleaning Check List

Friday – Cleaning Tasks	✔

Saturday – Cleaning Tasks	✔

Sunday – Cleaning Tasks	✔

Plans for Next Week:

NOTES:

_____

_____

_____

_____

My Weekly Cleaning Check List

This Weeks' To Do List:

1)
2)
3)
4)
5)

My Personal Goals This Week:

My Daily Cleaning Check List

WEEK BEGINNING:

DAILY TASK:	MON	TUES	WED	THURS	FRI	SAT	SUN

DATES TO REMEMBER THIS WEEK:

CLEANING SUPPLIES NEEDED:

My Weekly Cleaning Check List

Monday – Cleaning Tasks	✓

Tuesday – Cleaning Tasks	✓

Wednesday – Cleaning Tasks	✓

Thursday – Cleaning Tasks	✓

NOTES:

_____

_____

_____

_____

My Weekly Cleaning Check List

Friday – Cleaning Tasks	✔

Saturday – Cleaning Tasks	✔

Sunday – Cleaning Tasks	✔

Plans for Next Week:

NOTES:

My Weekly Cleaning Check List

This Weeks' To Do List:

1)
2)
3)
4)
5)

My Personal Goals This Week:

My Daily Cleaning Check List

WEEK BEGINNING:

DAILY TASK:	MON	TUES	WED	THURS	FRI	SAT	SUN

DATES TO REMEMBER THIS WEEK:

CLEANING SUPPLIES NEEDED:

My Weekly Cleaning Check List

Monday – Cleaning Tasks	✓

Tuesday – Cleaning Tasks	✓

Wednesday – Cleaning Tasks	✓

Thursday – Cleaning Tasks	✓

NOTES:

_____

_____

_____

_____

My Weekly Cleaning Check List

Friday – Cleaning Tasks	✔

Saturday – Cleaning Tasks	✔

Sunday – Cleaning Tasks	✔

Plans for Next Week:

NOTES:

_____

_____

_____

_____

My Weekly Cleaning Check List

This Weeks' To Do List:

1)
2)
3)
4)
5)

My Personal Goals This Week:

My Daily Cleaning Check List

WEEK BEGINNING:

DAILY TASK:	MON	TUES	WED	THURS	FRI	SAT	SUN

DATES TO REMEMBER THIS WEEK:

CLEANING SUPPLIES NEEDED:

My Weekly Cleaning Check List

Monday – Cleaning Tasks	✔

Tuesday – Cleaning Tasks	✔

Wednesday – Cleaning Tasks	✔

Thursday – Cleaning Tasks	✔

NOTES:

_____

_____

_____

_____

My Weekly Cleaning Check List

Friday – Cleaning Tasks	✔

Saturday – Cleaning Tasks	✔

Sunday – Cleaning Tasks	✔

Plans for Next Week:

NOTES:

_____

_____

_____

_____

My Weekly Cleaning Check List

This Weeks' To Do List:

1)	
2)	
3)	
4)	
5)	

My Personal Goals This Week:

My Daily Cleaning Check List

WEEK BEGINNING:

DAILY TASK:	MON	TUES	WED	THURS	FRI	SAT	SUN

DATES TO REMEMBER THIS WEEK:

CLEANING SUPPLIES NEEDED:

My Weekly Cleaning Check List

Monday – Cleaning Tasks	✔

Tuesday – Cleaning Tasks	✔

Wednesday – Cleaning Tasks	✔

Thursday – Cleaning Tasks	✔

NOTES:

_____

_____

_____

_____

My Weekly Cleaning Check List

Friday – Cleaning Tasks	✔

Saturday – Cleaning Tasks	✔

Sunday – Cleaning Tasks	✔

Plans for Next Week:

NOTES:

_____

_____

_____

_____

My Weekly Cleaning Check List

This Weeks' To Do List:

1)
2)
3)
4)
5)

My Personal Goals This Week:

My Daily Cleaning Check List

WEEK BEGINNING:

DAILY TASK:	MON	TUES	WED	THURS	FRI	SAT	SUN

DATES TO REMEMBER THIS WEEK:

CLEANING SUPPLIES NEEDED:

My Weekly Cleaning Check List

Monday – Cleaning Tasks	✓

Tuesday – Cleaning Tasks	✓

Wednesday – Cleaning Tasks	✓

Thursday – Cleaning Tasks	✓

NOTES:

_____

_____

_____

_____

My Weekly Cleaning Check List

Friday – Cleaning Tasks	✓

Saturday – Cleaning Tasks	✓

Sunday – Cleaning Tasks	✓

Plans for Next Week:

NOTES:

_____

_____

_____

_____

My Weekly Cleaning Check List

This Weeks' To Do List:

1)
2)
3)
4)
5)

My Personal Goals This Week:

My Daily Cleaning Check List

WEEK BEGINNING:

DAILY TASK:	MON	TUES	WED	THURS	FRI	SAT	SUN

DATES TO REMEMBER THIS WEEK:

CLEANING SUPPLIES NEEDED:

My Weekly Cleaning Check List

Monday – Cleaning Tasks	✔

Tuesday – Cleaning Tasks	✔

Wednesday – Cleaning Tasks	✔

Thursday – Cleaning Tasks	✔

NOTES:

_____

_____

_____

_____

My Weekly Cleaning Check List

Friday – Cleaning Tasks	✓

Saturday – Cleaning Tasks	✓

Sunday – Cleaning Tasks	✓

Plans for Next Week:

NOTES:

_____

_____

_____

_____

My Weekly Cleaning Check List

This Weeks' To Do List:

1)
2)
3)
4)
5)

My Personal Goals This Week:

My Daily Cleaning Check List

WEEK BEGINNING:

DAILY TASK:	MON	TUES	WED	THURS	FRI	SAT	SUN

DATES TO REMEMBER THIS WEEK:

CLEANING SUPPLIES NEEDED:

My Weekly Cleaning Check List

Monday – Cleaning Tasks	✓

Tuesday – Cleaning Tasks	✓

Wednesday – Cleaning Tasks	✓

Thursday – Cleaning Tasks	✓

NOTES:

_____

_____

_____

_____

My Weekly Cleaning Check List

Friday – Cleaning Tasks	✔

Saturday – Cleaning Tasks	✔

Sunday – Cleaning Tasks	✔

Plans for Next Week:

NOTES:

My Weekly Cleaning Check List

This Weeks' To Do List:

1)
2)
3)
4)
5)

My Personal Goals This Week:

My Daily Cleaning Check List

WEEK BEGINNING:

DAILY TASK:	MON	TUES	WED	THURS	FRI	SAT	SUN

DATES TO REMEMBER THIS WEEK:

CLEANING SUPPLIES NEEDED:

My Weekly Cleaning Check List

Monday – Cleaning Tasks	✓

Tuesday – Cleaning Tasks	✓

Wednesday – Cleaning Tasks	✓

Thursday – Cleaning Tasks	✓

NOTES:

_____

_____

_____

_____

My Weekly Cleaning Check List

Friday – Cleaning Tasks	✔

Saturday – Cleaning Tasks	✔

Sunday – Cleaning Tasks	✔

Plans for Next Week:

NOTES:

_____

_____

_____

_____

My Weekly Cleaning Check List

This Weeks' To Do List:

1)
2)
3)
4)
5)

My Personal Goals This Week:

My Daily Cleaning Check List

WEEK BEGINNING:

DAILY TASK:	MON	TUES	WED	THURS	FRI	SAT	SUN

DATES TO REMEMBER THIS WEEK:

CLEANING SUPPLIES NEEDED:

My Weekly Cleaning Check List

Monday – Cleaning Tasks	✓

Tuesday – Cleaning Tasks	✓

Wednesday – Cleaning Tasks	✓

Thursday – Cleaning Tasks	✓

NOTES:

_____

_____

_____

_____

My Weekly Cleaning Check List

Friday – Cleaning Tasks	✔

Saturday – Cleaning Tasks	✔

Sunday – Cleaning Tasks	✔

Plans for Next Week:

NOTES:

_____

_____

_____

_____

My Weekly Cleaning Check List

This Weeks' To Do List:

1)
2)
3)
4)
5)

My Personal Goals This Week:

My Daily Cleaning Check List

WEEK BEGINNING:

DAILY TASK:	MON	TUES	WED	THURS	FRI	SAT	SUN

DATES TO REMEMBER THIS WEEK:

CLEANING SUPPLIES NEEDED:

My Weekly Cleaning Check List

Monday – Cleaning Tasks	✓

Tuesday – Cleaning Tasks	✓

Wednesday – Cleaning Tasks	✓

Thursday – Cleaning Tasks	✓

NOTES:

_____

_____

_____

_____

My Weekly Cleaning Check List

Friday – Cleaning Tasks	✔

Saturday – Cleaning Tasks	✔

Sunday – Cleaning Tasks	✔

Plans for Next Week:

NOTES:

My Weekly Cleaning Check List

This Weeks' To Do List:

1)	
2)	
3)	
4)	
5)	

My Personal Goals This Week:

My Monthly Cleaning Check List

CLEANING TASK	JAN	FEB	MAR	APRIL	MAY	JUNE

My Monthly Cleaning Check List

CLEANING TASK	JULY	AUG	SEPT	OCT	NOV	DEC

My Monthly Cleaning Check List

CLEANING TASK	JAN	FEB	MAR	APRIL	MAY	JUNE

My Monthly Cleaning Check List

CLEANING TASK	JULY	AUG	SEPT	OCT	NOV	DEC

Ideas for Check Lists

Daily Suggestions:

Clean Kitchen Counter Tops	Empty and Reload Dishwasher
Put on Load of Laundry and Dry	Make Beds
General Pick Up	Vacuum Kitchen Floor
Fold Laundry	Put Clean Clothes Away
Wipe Toilets	Put Out Recycling

Weekly Suggestions:

Vacuum Living Room	Clean Bathrooms
Vacuum Stairs and Hallways	Strip Beds
Wash Towels	Vacuum Bed Rooms
Wipe and Clean Doors	Food Shopping
Clear out Fridge	Empty Bins
Dusting	Wash Tea Towels and Cloths
Mop Kitchen Floor	Clean Stove Top
Clean Microwave	Clean Kitchen Cabinets

Ideas for Check Lists

Monthly Suggestions:

Vacuum Sofa	Clean out and Sort Through Cupboards
Clean Porch	Vacuum Underneath Beds
Test Smoke Detectors	Clean Refrigerator
Clean Oven and Ovenhood	Wipe Blinds / Curtains
Clean Baseboards	Wash out Trash Cans / Bins
Wash Rugs	Go Through Wardrobes / Clothes
Clean Windows	Wipe and Clean Window Sills
Polish Glass	Wash Cushion Covers
Dusting	Sweep Driveway
Sort Through and Straighten Shoes	Clean Mirrors
Dust Pictures	Vacuum around edges and corners of room
Clean Small Appliances	Run Empty Dishwasher with Vinegar or Dishwasher Cleaner
Wash Showerhead	Clean Ceiling Fans
Wipe Down Electronic Devices	Wipe and Clean Switches

Thank you for using Your Daily, Weekly and Monthly Cleaning Planner

I sincerely hope that you have enjoyed using it and that you have found it has made your cleaning more efficient and stress-free.

I would love to hear what you think. Please spare the time to leave me a review on Amazon. Simply search for this Planner –

"Your Daily, Weekly and Monthly Cleaning Planner" by Family and Household Planner Company

Your reviews help me enormously – thank you!

Jennifer Clarke

Printed in Great Britain
by Amazon